THE 9 HABITS OF LAWS OF LEADERSHIP

Highly effective strategy into becoming a good leader

By

Dr Stella hill

Copyright@ 2024.Dr.Stella Hill

ALL right reserved

TABLE OF CONTENT

- INTRODUCTION 4
  - Chapter 1 10
    - Laws of Self-Awareness and Understanding Others 10
  - Chapter 2 32
    - The law of transformed leadership 32
  - CHAPTER 3 48
    - Laws of Leadership: 48
  - CHAPTER 4 58
    - The laws of successful leadership 58
  - Chapter 5 74
    - Leadership skill that are still relevant in the AI Age 74
  - Chapter 6 88
    - The laws of respect 88
  - Chapter 7 102
    - Become a Stronger and More Effective Leader (Law of Process) 102
  - Chapter 8 116
    - Rules for good leadership 116
  - CHAPTER 9 134
    - conclusion 134

INTRODUCTION

Leadership is extremely important in both our personal and professional lives, much like the brilliant guiding star in the night sky. The best-selling control book ever reached a whole new level!

Ruth's New York Times best-seller, completely updated for its fifth anniversary, offers straightforward guidance on how to become a successful leader in the modern world.

You will examine the essential components of a hit management, which are vision, impact, accountability, and dedication. It emphasizes methods for creating objectives for both you and your organization while also maintaining emotional equilibrium throughout trying moments. Motivating and logical examples from Maxwell's personal experience support each law.

John Maxwell went above and above with every word in this book, updating it for the current generation of leaders with fresh perspectives on those ageless criminal advice and applying lessons learned from the fact that he originally penned the book. He erased old memories and replaced them with bright ones that reflect the modern business world.

The effective control realities that have helped people become better leaders for the last century are what he failed to change. Regardless of whether people need to: do independent research on leadership; teach management to others as a mentor; it is still the excellent e-book on management that people should buy.

I am alive. It is the engine that drives creativity, expansion, and constructive change, launching people, groups, and companies toward success. In whatever area of life, be it business, politics, sports, or any other, good leadership is essential to influencing the present and creating a better future.

Fundamentally, leadership is about motivating and persuading others to accomplish a shared objective. It is the capacity to lead people toward a common goal and enable them to reach their greatest potential. Gaining proficiency in fundamental concepts and techniques is necessary for the trans-formative journey of becoming an extraordinary leader. There are probably more than ten attributes that come to mind when asked to describe the characteristics of a leader. This blog will draw inspiration from Daniel Lee's book "First Time Leadership," which distills these behaviors into five rules of leadership that help people become effective leaders. Aspiring leaders can realize their full leadership potential and encourage others to do the same by emphasizing self-awareness, emotional intelligence, compassion, teamwork, and trust-building. Let us examine these laws and see why anyone hoping to be a successful leader has to know them!

Fundamentally, leadership is about motivating and persuading others to accomplish a shared objective. It is the capacity to lead people toward a common goal and enable them to reach their greatest potential. Gaining proficiency in fundamental concepts and techniques is necessary for the trans-formative journey of becoming an extraordinary leader. There are probably more than ten attributes that come to mind when asked to describe the characteristics of a leader. This blog will draw inspiration from Daniel Lee's book "First Time Leadership," which distills these behaviors into five rules of leadership that help people become effective leaders.

Dr Stella Hill

Chapter 1

Laws of Self-Awareness and Understanding Others.

Do you want to be a more contented person, more powerful, better decision-maker, and more successful leader? Therefore, the most crucial skill to master is self-awareness. It is what will enable you to stay focused on being the greatest leader and self-actualize r you can be. The advantages of self-awareness are as unique as each person; some examples are improved perspective, more influence, and more solid interpersonal bonds. Let us examine self-awareness, its definitions, and methods for growth.

What is self-awareness? Self-awareness is defined as "conscious knowledge of one's own character, feelings, motives, and desires," according to Oxford Language. Psychologists Shelley Du-val and Robert Wicklund proposed this definition: "Self-awareness is the ability to focus on yourself and how your actions, thoughts, or emotions do or don't align with your internal standards. If you're highly self-aware, you can objectively evaluate yourself, manage your emotions, align your behavior with your values, and understand correctly how others perceive you." Put simply, those who are highly self-aware can interpret their actions, feelings, and thoughts objectively. It's a rare skill, as many of us spiral into emotion-driven interpretations of our circumstances. Developing self-awareness is important because it allows leaders to assess their growth and effectiveness and change course when necessary.

Types of self-awareness

There are two distinct kinds of self-awareness, public and private.

Public self-awareness: Being aware of how we can appear to others. Because of this consciousness, we are more likely to adhere to social norms and behave in ways that are socially acceptable.

While there are benefits to this type of awareness, there is also the danger of tipping into self-consciousness. Those who are especially high in this trait may spend too much time worrying about what others think of them. Private self-awareness: Being able to notice and reflect on one's internal state. Those who have private self-awareness are introspective, approaching their feelings and reactions with curiosity.

For example, you may notice yourself tensing up as you are preparing for an important meeting. Noticing the physical sensations and correctly attributing them to your anxiety about the meeting would be an example of private self-awareness. When self-awareness tips into self-consciousness, we are reluctant to share certain aspects of ourselves. We develop a persona that lacks authenticity.

Why is self-awareness important?

The Eu-rich group has researched the nature of self-awareness. Their research indicates that when we look inward, we can clarify our values, thoughts, feelings, behaviors, strengths, and weaknesses. We are able to recognize the effect that we have on others. Eu rich's research finds that people with self-awareness are happier and have better relationships. They also experience a sense of personal and social control as well as higher job satisfaction.

When we look outward, we understand how people view us. People who are aware of how people see them are more likely to be empathetic to people with different perspectives. Leaders whose self-perception matches others' perceptions are more likely to empower, include, and recognize others.

Benefits of self-awareness

As we mentioned earlier, strengthening self-awareness has a variety of benefits. The specifics of each one depends on the individual.

Here are some examples of common benefits of self-awareness: •

1. It gives us the power to influence outcomes

It helps us to become better decision-makers It gives us more self-confidence — so, as a result, we communicate with clarity and intention. •

2. It allows us to understand things from multiple perspectives •
3. It frees us from our assumptions and biases. •
4. It helps us build better relationships. •
5. It gives us a greater ability to regulate our emotions. •It decreases stress. •
6. It makes us happier.

What's the self-awareness gap?

Self-awareness is a staple in contemporary leadership jargon. Although many leaders will brag about how self-aware they are, only 10 to 15 percent of the population fit the criteria. Many of us grew up with the message that you should not show your emotions, so we attempt to ignore or suppress them. With negative emotions, that doesn't go very well for us. We either internalize them (resulting in anger, resentment, depression, and resignation) or we externalize them and blame, discount, or bully others.

Lack of self-awareness can be a significant handicap in leadership. A study conducted by Adam D. Kandinsky and colleagues at North-western's Kellogg School of Management found that often, as executives climb the corporate ladder, they become more self-assured and confident. On the downside, they tend to become more self-absorbed and less likely to consider the perspectives of others.

In a separate study, Canadian researchers looked at brain activity in people who are in positions of power. They found physiological evidence to conclude that as power increases, the ability to empathize with others decreases. They become less able to consider the needs and perspectives of others. Fundamentally these leaders don't think they need to change and instead require a change from everyone else.

How do I know if I'm a self-aware person?

Don't despair if you don't make the 10-15 percent self-awareness cut. If you want to know how self-aware you are, the iNLP Center has 12 multiple-choice questions that will tell you the level of your self-awareness and what you can do to improve it. The assessment is research-based and developed by Mike Bundrant, a neuron-linguistic trainer and life coach.

The Values in Action Inventory of Strengths (VIA-IS) is a great tool for you to use to identify your dominant strengths and is free on the VIA website. It measures your answers across six broad categories with a total of 24 strengths. Take the assessment, and you'll generate a report identifying your top 5 strengths and how to begin to optimize them.

How to become a more self-aware person

Envision yourself

Visualize the best version of yourself. "Ideal selves reflect our hopes, dreams, aspirations, and speak to our skills, abilities, achievements, and accomplishments that we wish to attain." (Higgins, 1987; Markus & Nurius, 1986.) As you lean into your strengths to become the better version of yourself, you can use this idealized self to keep moving in the right direction and not be distracted by setbacks and other obstacles.

Ask the "what" questions

At the core of self-awareness is the ability to self-reflect. However, the Eu-rich group contends that most people are going about reflection in the wrong way. The trouble is, we ask ourselves the wrong questions. In our attempt to resolve internal conflict, we ask, "Why?" Yet there's no way to answer that question since we don't have access to our unconscious. Instead, we make up answers that may not be accurate.

The danger of the "why" question is that it sends us down the rabbit hole of our negative thoughts. We focus on our weaknesses and insecurities. Consider Amy, a new junior executive who has difficulty speaking up at meetings. She may explain her experience to herself by thinking, "I don't speak up at meetings because I fall too low in the corporate food chain. No one's going to listen to me.

" Asking the "what question" puts us into the objective and open space of considering all the factors influencing a particular outcome. For

example, instead of "Why don't I speak up at meetings? we could ask: •

"What were the interpersonal dynamics in the room?" •

"What was I experiencing in my body at the time?" •

"What happened that caused me to go into my old story of not being good enough?" •

"What can I do to overcome my fear of speaking up?"

This kind of introspection allows us to look at behaviors and beliefs for what they are. With self-awareness, we can examine old patterns and stories that do not serve us, and then we can move on. Asking the right questions empowers us to make different choices that bring different results.

Amy decides to make a plan because now she understands that she has a chance at overcoming her problem.

She's going to find out more about the content and goals of an upcoming meeting to become more confident in how she can contribute. •

Rather than being consumed by imagining what others are thinking about her, she'll actively listen for cues to ask meaningful questions that move the conversation forward.

With a heightened awareness of the cues her body is giving her signaling fear and anxiety, she'll name the emotion at the moment and choose not to be overwhelmed by it — one giant

step to self-awareness.

Strengthen your brain

The amygdala, also called the primitive brain, was the first part of the brain to develop in humans. It functioned as a kind of radar signaling the need to run away or fight back. That part of the brain is skilled at anticipating danger and reacts before we can even name a negative emotion. Our heart races, our stomach tightens, and our neck muscles tense up.

Your body's reaction is a tripwire signaling the prefrontal cortex to register or name a negative emotion. If you bring awareness to your physical state, you can, at the moment, recognize the emotion as it is happening. Becoming skillful at this rewires your brain.

Naming your feelings is critical in decision-making. When we let our feelings overwhelm us, we can make bad decisions with unintended consequences. Naming your emotions allows us to take a "third-person" perspective to stand back and more objectively evaluate what's going on.

Let's bring this home with an example. You, a self-aware person, are having a conversation with someone and receiving some negative feedback. Your heart starts to race, and you're feeling threatened. You say to yourself, "I feel like this person is attacking me." But, before you cry or go ballistic, you stop yourself and hear the person out. You discover that this person had at least one good point and start up a different conversation, one that is mutually satisfying and productive.

Ask others about their perception of you.

Now that you've discovered that feedback doesn't have to be scary, ask other people how they perceive you in certain situations. Getting specific will help to give you the most concrete feedback. Get brave and ask them how they would like to see you behave.

Exercise: Pick out a scenario(s) you would like to receive

feedback on and list them. Make two columns.

Column A: How I see myself

Column B: How others see me.

In Column A make a list of words to describe your attitude and behaviors at the time.

Then, ask your feedback partner to do the same and record those responses in Column B. Look out for discrepancies. You may have some blind spots that need attending.

Keep a journal.

Journalism is a great way to pay attention to what's going on in your private and public self. It will also help you to recognize patterns that either serve you or not. You may use these prompts:

1. What did I do well today?

2. What challenges did I face?

3. What was I feeling?

4. How did I respond? In retrospect, would I have responded differently?

5. What strengths did I use to keep me focused on the best version of myself?

6. What is my intention for tomorrow?

Practice mindfulness

Mindfulness is a practice. It helps you be aware of what's going on in your mind, body, and environment. Meditation is one of a few practices that you can insert into your daily life, and practicing mindfulness is a wonderful tool for developing greater self-control.

Here are some ideas of mindfulness activities to get you started: •Practice deep breathing .

•Name you surroundings .

•Organize your space .

•Draw or paint .

The road to self-awareness is a journey. The most self-aware people see themselves on a quest to mastery rather than at a particular destination. As you move forward in developing your self-awareness, ask yourself regularly, "How will you move toward the best version of yourself today?"

Dr Stella Hill

Chapter 2

The law of transformed leadership

You don't have to spend long in the working world to recognize there are multiple types of leaders. Every kind of leader motivates, challenges and develops employees in different ways. Their corresponding styles can all inspire different outcomes. In recent years, transformed leader has risen to the surface. Organizations in all industries are seeing rapid change in today's digital era. Transformed leader know how to encourage, inspire and motivate employees to perform in ways that create meaningful change.

The result is an engaged workforce that's empowered to innovate and help shape an organization's future success. Your curiosity may leave you wondering, "What is transformed leader, exactly?" Join us as we help answer this question.

The origins of transformed leader

While transformed leader principles are well-suited for today's fast-paced, diverse and highly technological workforce, the style is far from a new development. Presidential biographer and leadership expert James MacGregor Burns is credited with coining the concept in the 1970s. Organizational change and leadership development expert Kevin Ford builds off this model that Burns initially identified. According to Ford, there are three effective leadership styles:

- Tactical leaders focus on solving straightforward problems with operations-oriented expertise.

- Strategic leaders are very future-focused with an ability to maintain a specific vision while forecasting industry and market trends.

- Transformed leader focus less on making decisions or establishing strategic plans, and more on facilitating organizational collaboration that can help drive a vision forward.

As you gain a clearer understanding of transformed leadership, it's helpful to walk through the various components that are inherent to this management style.

4 Components of transformed leaders

As transformed leaders work with their employees to implement effective change, they rely on things like communication, charisma, adaptability and empathetic support. In practice, this leadership style comprises four primary elements:

- Individualized consideration — Transformed leaders listen to employees' concerns and needs so they can provide adequate support. They operate from the understanding that what motivates one person may not motivate someone else. As a result, they're able to adapt their management styles to accommodate various individuals on their team.

• •Inspirational motivation — Transformed leaders are able to articulate a unified vision that encourages team members to exceed expectations. They understand that the most motivated employees are the ones who have a strong sense of purpose. These leaders are not afraid to challenge employees. They remain optimistic about future goals and are skilled at giving meaning to the tasks at hand. •

•Idealized influence — Transformed leaders model ethical behavior. Their moral conduct earns a necessary level of respect and trust. This can help leaders steer decision-making that works to improve the entire organization.

•Intellectual stimulation — Transformed leaders regularly challenge assumptions, take risks and solicit team members' input and ideas. They don't fear failure, and instead foster an environment where it's safe to have conversations, be creative and voice diverse perspectives. This empowers employees to ask questions, practice a greater level of autonomy and ultimately determine more effective ways to execute their tasks.

Transformed leaders is a powerful management methodology backed by decades of research. Transformed leaders improve outcomes related to the following:

Effectiveness and performance.

•Creativity and innovation.

•Well-being and motivation.

•Satisfaction and commitment.

•Engagement, trust, and communication.

Despite the introduction of new leadership models and theories over the past 40 years since the emergence of transformed leadership, researchers have found that many borrow from its focus on social influence tactics. This replication lends credence to transformed leadership's validity as a fundamental set of principles that make sense and produce beneficial results across an organization.

A recommended leadership style.

The American Nurses Credentialing Center (ANCC) recommends the transformed leadership style for hospitals seeking to achieve their Magnet® designation. The model's focus on continual process improvement aligns well with nurses' constant need to change and adapt to new developments in health care.

Felicia Saddler, MJ, BSN, RN, CPHQ, LSSBB, Vice President of Quality at Relias, affirmed that even if the transformed leadership style does not feel natural, individuals at all levels can take steps to incorporate qualities and characteristics associated with transformed leaders into their professional practice.

Starting the journey to transformed leadership.

Start by taking a personal inventory of your current strengths, weaknesses, and natural leadership style to determine what you need to learn to start your journey to transformed leadership.

Anyone can adopt the transformed leadership style by reflecting on their attitudes and mindset. In addition, you can put these four core elements of the transformed leadership model into action

: 1. Idealized influence.

2. Inspirational motivation.

3. Individualized consideration

4. Intellectual stimulation.

First Step: Idealized Impact

Idealized influence refers to a leader's capacity to uplift others and function as an exemplar of exceptional professional conduct. Employees respect and trust such a boss.

A nurse leader who promotes open communication, for instance, can set an example for this trait by hosting team meetings at the beginning of each shift. These are occasions for the leader to show effective communication skills and to encourage staff members to share their experiences, raise issues, and offer solutions.

How to put it into practice:

❖❖❖ Means are not as powerful as actions. Showcase the conduct you desire people to emulate. Show people how you want them to behave instead of just telling them.

❖❖❖ Pay attention to what other people are doing right rather than their flaws. Be upbeat whenever you can.

Never underestimate the impact of expressing gratitude. Including details will help the behavior you wish to be repeated.

Please provide comments.

- Acknowledge challenging circumstances.

Utilize the assets of others.

- Remember the three "Bs": Be nice. Be reliable. Make yourself known.

Step 2: Motivational Inspiration

The ability of a leader to convey a vision that people can relate to and want to join is known as inspirational motivation. It creates a sense of purpose by bringing corporate and individual goals into alignment.

A hospital administrator, for instance, can come up with innovative strategies to motivate employees by sharing their future vision. One idea would be to get together in groups with the staff to develop goals.

How to put it into practice:

Assist others in understanding the big picture and provide justifications.

Refrain from micromanaging. Give individuals the freedom to "go do" instead. Give your staff the latitude to achieve the goals because there are multiple approaches to completing a task.

❖❖❖ Consider what motivates your staff, keeping in mind that this will vary over time. Ask those you speak with what their goals are.

Tailor awards and recognition to maintain employee engagement.

The 9 habits of laws of leadership

Dr Stella Hill

CHAPTER 3

Laws of Leadership:

Leadership, like the bright guiding star in a night sky, carries enormous importance in our personal and professional life. It is the force that propels individuals, teams, and organizations toward success, generating innovation, growth, and positive change. In whatever area of life, be it business, politics, sports, or any other, good leadership is essential to influencing the present and creating a better future.

Fundamentally, leadership is about motivating and persuading others to accomplish a shared objective. It is the capacity to lead people toward a common goal and enable them to reach their greatest potential. It takes a transforming journey to become an exceptional leader, requiring the mastery of fundamental concepts and practices. There are probably more than ten attributes that come to mind when asked to describe the characteristics of a leader. This blog will draw inspiration from Daniel Lee's book "First Time Leadership," which condenses these behaviors into five rules of leadership that open doors for people to become powerful leaders. Aspiring leaders can realize their full leadership potential and encourage others to do the same by emphasizing self-awareness, emotional intelligence, compassion, teamwork, and trust-building. Let us examine these laws and see why anyone hoping to be a successful leader has to know them!

1. Show courage. Show kindness.

2. I will be talking (and writing!) about this a lot, and for good reason—the most effective leaders are those who forge ahead and are not afraid to take on challenges that others won't. When you take that risk, you will be amazed at what you can achieve! Always behave bravely and with kindness.

I Trust your gut feeling, but do not ignore what other people have to say.

Why should anybody else have faith in you and your actions if you are unable to trust your instincts? While it is necessary to carefully weigh all possibilities and consequences before making a decision, great leaders are known for their ability to make the right decisions and keep people and organizations out of difficulty. This is not to say that you should disregard what other people believe. Although it can be difficult, you must learn to trust yourself if you want to improve as a leader.

2. Always show respect

A leader who does not show respect to others will never gain that respect, nor will they be able to get the most out of their team. Since respect is the foundation of all interactions, developing relationships at work is essential to success.

3. Have an empowering attitude

Giving others around you the support and resources they need to succeed pushes them to achieve their goals and fosters a sense of pride in their work and self-worth. In addition to making you feel good, making other people happy will improve the atmosphere at work. Additionally, you will enhance the company's culture, which will benefit the entire organization.

4. Set an example for what you expect from other people.

Leaders who practice "do as I say, not as I do" lack respect and will soon destroy a pleasant work environment. It is essential that you set an example for your team by modeling honesty, hard effort, and dedication. Since enthusiasm is contagious, share it with your team and watch the positive effects.

5. Be prepared to follow morality even in the face of opposition from others.

A crucial quality shared by all outstanding leaders is their honesty and their commitment to following their moral convictions. Without someone taking the chance, speaking up, and declaring "No more," no significant change could ever be done. This is the proper course of action. Even if some people might not agree with you, you will almost certainly win their respect if you do not waver and always do the right thing, no matter how difficult it is.

Never give up learning.

It is a fact of life that you will never know everything. However, things are continually changing; new technology or research is released, and in order to keep ahead of the competition, you must always be studying and looking for new knowledge. Gaining more expertise and understanding is always beneficial.

These are the rules I live by every day, and I hope they encourage you to advance and become a more capable leader.

Top 3 reason why you may choose to adopt these laws of leadership

1. **Unlock Your Leadership Potential**. Embracing the Laws of Leadership opens the door to unlocking your full

leadership potential. By cultivating self-awareness, emotional intelligence, compassion, collaboration, and trust-building, you tap into the essential qualities that make a great leader. These laws provide a road-map for personal and professional growth, allowing you to develop the skills, mindset, and behaviors necessary to lead with excellence.

2. Drive Team Success and Engagement. Implementing the Laws of Leadership positively impacts your team's success and engagement. When you prioritize self-awareness, emotional intelligence, compassion, collaboration, and trust-building, you create a supportive and empowering environment. This fosters stronger relationships, enhances communication, and cultivates a sense of purpose and fulfillment among team members.

By embodying these laws, you inspire your team to perform at their best, driving productivity, innovation, and overall success.

3. Build Strong and Lasting Relationships. Effective leadership is built on trust, respect, and strong relationships. By embracing the 5 Laws of Leadership, you prioritize trust-building, empathy, collaboration, and open communication. This not only strengthens your relationships with team members but also builds trust and credibility among peers, superiors, and stakeholders. Strong relationships are the foundation of successful leadership, enabling you to influence, inspire, and garner support from others. Adopting the these laws of leadership as your guiding principles can revolutionize your leadership approach. By mastering self-awareness, emotional intelligence, compassion, collaboration, and trust-building, you create an environment that fosters growth, innovation, and team excellence. These laws empower leaders to inspire and motivate their team members, driving them towards exceptional results.

Chapter 4

The laws of successful leadership

Whether they are aware of it or not, effective leaders adhere to a set of rules.

Working with extraordinarily successful people over the years has shown me that, in order to construct your exterior reality, your internal beliefs must be addressed if you want to succeed at anything. Being at your best in all facets of your life—not just your career—is the key to success.

I have found that the following common principles apply to actually attaining success. You can quickly build whatever it is you want to make if you read these laws often until they become second nature.

1. Show consideration for the worldviews of others.

Everybody has an internal world, and these worlds are very distinct from one another. When you accept that other people will not always say or do what you agree with, you will find a great deal of clarity and freedom. You will gain a deeper understanding of someone and establish a stronger connection with them. The other person will also feel appreciated and understood if you do this. People that are successful are able to deal with a wide variety of people and traverse their various models.

2 Dismantle obstacles that impede progress.

There are no genuinely resistant individuals in the world.

You have not developed enough rapport with people in your life if you feel that they are resisting you, whether they be family members, business associates, or anybody else. Your relationships will get easier the more you learn to connect with people and develop empathy naturally. Reach out to individuals on their terms. Assimilate their communication style and want to establish a more meaningful relationship.

3. Recognize that individuals are not their actions.

Someone is actions or words do not always reflect who they are as a person. You will begin to see that people's acts are wholly distinct from who they are once you start to divorce people from their behaviors. You will begin to see that there is space for development and progress and begin to judge less. Instead of focusing on a person's characteristics, successful people help others with their behaviors.

4. Recognize that people make the greatest effort they can with the tools at their disposal.

Recognize that the person you are interacting with is making every effort to the best of their ability with the resources at their disposal at the moment. Even if they might be getting less than ideal results, know that they are giving it their all. For instance, you may not have been aware of all these regulations prior to reading this post, but now that you are, you may utilize them to your advantage to get better outcomes.

Continue making investments in fresh tools to support your positive transformation if you want to maintain your personal success. Success does not just happen to people. They do not simply exist in a world where everything occurs on autopilot and they have no idea how they got there.

5. Take charge of your outcomes.

You are responsible for all that you currently have or do not have in your life. It is the result of the attitudes, ideas, deeds, and behaviors you engage in on a regular basis. People who are successful do not function from a victim mentality. They do not think, "I wish I had that," or "I wish this was happening in this particular way." The concept of wish is nonexistent. Everything that you have done in the past is directly reflected in what you have. It is your responsibility to alter the result. It is a really powerful place to be once you really begin living by this commandment every day.

6. **Aim to be complete.**

Your goal should be to become more wholehearted in all that you do in life. The key is to strike a balance. For instance, a person may be financially successful but physically unfit. Alternatively, you may have all the money in the world, but you could not enjoy it if you did not have connections or your health. This should be the goal of every choice you make, action you do, and discussion you have. In the end, you are dying if you are not evolving.

7. Assess your impact.

Examine the quality of your talks or connection if you are trying to influence, bargain, or converse with someone and you are not liking the answer you are getting. Ultimately, you can always modify your inquiries if you are not satisfied with the answer you are receiving in a relationship—or even in a particular aspect of your life.

8. Show adaptability.

You will experience setbacks, bumps on the road, and ups and downs in life. It all depends on how you choose to respond to whatever life throws at you, regardless of the cause. Be adaptable and consider how you react to situations that help you achieve your desired outcomes.

I urge you to familiarize yourself with these regulations; you can even print them off, post them on your wall, and forward them to your friends. Begin implementing these laws in your daily life to experience success.

The Greatest Advice From Agency Leaders For New Colleagues

Long-term success for those new to the fields of PR, marketing, and advertising depends on matching their thoughts, deeds, and behaviors to the demands of their company and the vision of its leaders. Through exhibiting a comprehension of and dedication to the organization's objectives, they establish themselves as significant assets and augment their prospects of progressing within the sector.

The TMS Agency Council members each offer their best tip for assisting a new agency teammate in assimilating into the

operation smoothly and quickly, ensuring that their efforts contribute meaningfully to the organization's objectives. Read on to learn how they recommend a rookie professional approach the on-boarding process to ensure their actions and outlook reflect the agency's core values. 1. Be Proactive Instead Of Reactionary First, be human and enjoy having a sense of purpose. Being afraid to fail will hold you back. Communicate your ideas, poke holes in them and then, if your approach still has legs, implement them. Shifting the work paradigm from being reactionary to being proactive will change your work experience from stressful to joyful. 2. You Don't Need To Have All The Answers You may not have all the answers for every client, and that's okay. We intentionally hire team members with complementary backgrounds and skill sets so that we can always crowd-source and pull in the expertise that's needed, no matter what our clients need. 3. Always Be Curious Our top piece of advice for brand-new employees who join the team is to always be curious. While they may have been hired for one role, we encourage them to learn others and grow internally. Learning the ecosystem is key to all of our success, and instilling that mindset aligns with our belief in a well-rounded organization and a team that is always learning and building internal relationships. - 4. Be You We hired you, not a "yes man" or a robot worker; we hired a human with thoughts, emotions, experience and a voice. Bring a new worldview or perspective to a project or initiative. Yes, fellow creatives can be competitive, but be willing to learn and be confident in what you know and your experiences. We are transparent and honest with the entire team, nurturing an environment of honesty. Ask Questions Our agency values continuous learning and collaboration, and your curiosity drives innovation. By seeking to understand not just the "what," but also the "why" behind our strategies, you'll quickly align with our mission to deliver thoughtful, impact work. This mindset ensures you contribute meaningfully from day one. - 6. Be Accountable A core element of our values is accountability. At our agency, this means honoring commitments through communication, adhering to deadlines and delivering expected results to both teammates and clients. Effective team members take responsibility for their actions and proactively communicate if they encounter obstacles in meeting deadlines.

7. Be Resourceful It is critical for success in the agency world that all team members be resourceful, seeking out the information to make decisions and overturning every rock to make informed recommendations to clients. Clients look to us for objective perspectives, and we must continually deliver 8. Remember That You Don't Know What You Don't Know My advice is to remember that you don't know what you don't know. Don't be afraid of

not knowing something. Ask questions or seek answers; it's okay not to know everything. This reflects our core value of authenticity. We are always honest with our clients about what we know, and we commit to figuring out what we don't. This approach builds trust and shows our dedication to continuous improvement. - 9. Embrace Our Culture Of Giving My top advice for a new employee is to embrace our culture of giving first. This approach has always been our way of doing things, and we were thrilled to see it best described in Adam Grant's book Give and Take. Building relationships through generosity and contribution is the core of our success, internally and with our clients. We want givers, not takers, on our team. 10. Always Ask Why Asking why helps you understand your role and the work we do, and it empowers you to respectfully challenge current processes. By asking why, you contribute to a culture of learning, shared insights and continuous improvement. This mindset is so vital to us that "Ask why" is one of our core values, ensuring we all grow and innovate together. 11. Never Make Assumptions My top piece of advice for a brand-new employee joining my agency is never to make assumptions. Time is money, and it's better to ask clarifying questions so that work is on-brand and on-purpose. We are paid equally to how much we are willing to think, and thinking doesn't happen in a silo. Be curious and communicative! - 12. Speak Your Mind The last thing that we (or any agency) needs is another "yes person" who is unwilling to argue, push back or ask questions to make ideas and strategies better. We will not always agree, and that's okay—90% of the time this is where great ideas come from. But if anyone new to our team has a legit concern or alternative idea, we want it brought to the table. 13. Connect With People We always, always say, "Relationship trumps transaction." So, when a new member joins the ECHO team, our first piece of advice is to connect with people. Share your stories, and listen to others' stories. Ask for help, and offer your help. Whatever form that exchange takes, it's a reflection of something we call "unconventional caring," which is one of our core values. It builds trust and sets people up for success.

14. Always Be Honest My top advice for new employees is to always be honest, even if mistakes happen. Don't make decisions in isolation. This reflects our core value of integrity. Transparency builds trust and encourages collaboration, helping us effectively address challenges.

Remember, seeking help is a strength, and by working together, we achieve the best outcomes for our clients. 15. Expect A Fast Pace To Get Faster Expect a fast pace in the beginning—before it gets faster. However, our on-boarding process is designed to prepare you with input, guidance and a road-map for success. As you transition from on-boarding to "on board," that guidance and road-map will still apply to each level of development you reach. This is in the firm's DNA: It's designed to enable you to perform at a higher level to reach the achievements you seek.

Chapter 5

Leadership skill that are still relevant in the AI Age

Artificial intelligence has the power to automate and streamline countless business processes and improve efficiency across just about every sector. However, AI tools (and the humans using them) need guidance and training to perform to their full potential, which makes strong leadership more important than ever. The members of some high rated company development council discuss the leadership skills that are still relevant in the age of AI. From strong critical thinking skills to communication and empathy, these traits are crucial to leading any organization through the transitions that come with new technology. 1. Emotional Intelligence In a rapidly evolving world, emotional intelligence is a crucial leadership skill, as it requires an understanding of the nuance that AI lacks. Leaders with a high EQ are self-aware, empathetic and reflective, which empowers them to navigate social complexities and manage relationships effectively, leading to better business outcomes and higher employee satisfaction. - 2. Empathy Our research shows that 68% of business leaders believe that today's work environment demands new leadership styles. In the age of AI, adaptability and empathy are critical. Adaptability enables leaders to swiftly respond to the rapidly changing AI landscape. Empathy helps leaders support employees as they navigate with active listening, investing in ongoing learning and encouraging a growth mindset. 3. Transparency The AI hype cycle has many people looking over their shoulders and fearing for their job security. As leaders, it is more important than ever to be transparent about how and why you plan to incorporate the use of AI into your business. You need your team working with you on these initiatives, not avoiding them out of fear of the unknown. -

4. The Ability To Identify Areas For Improvement With AI, leaders now have the ability to create bespoke coaching for any skill they want to improve. Want to become a better listener? Chatting will happily create a plan with tactics and exercises to help you develop that skill. Wondering how to deal with a difficult situation? It's likely that AI can summarize the world's knowledge on the subject. It's a brave new world. 5. A Commitment

To Continuous Learning In the age of artificial intelligence, adaptability is the most relevant leadership principle. Leaders can develop this skill by staying updated on AI advancements, embracing continuous learning and promoting a culture of innovation. This adaptability enables leaders to integrate AI effectively, enhancing decision-making and driving career growth. 2. Empathy Our research shows that 68% of business leaders believe that today's work environment demands new leadership styles. In the age of AI, adaptability and empathy are critical. Adaptability enables leaders to swiftly respond to the rapidly changing AI landscape. Empathy helps leaders support employees as they navigate with active listening, investing in ongoing learning and encouraging a growth mindset. 3. Transparency The AI hype cycle has many people looking over their shoulders and fearing for their job security. As leaders, it is more important than ever to be transparent about how and why you plan to incorporate the use of AI into your business. You need your team working with you on these initiatives, not avoiding them out of fear of the unknown. 4. The Ability To Identify Areas For Improvement With AI, leaders now have the ability to create bespoke coaching for any skill they want to improve. Want to become a better listener? Chatting will happily create a plan with tactics and exercises to help you develop that skill. Wondering how to deal with a difficult situation? It's likely that AI can summarize the world's knowledge on the subject. It's a brave new world.

5. **A Commitment** To Continuous Learning In the age of artificial intelligence, adaptability is the most relevant

leadership principle. Leaders can develop this skill by staying updated on AI advancements, embracing continuous learning and promoting a culture of innovation. This adaptability enables leaders to integrate AI effectively, enhancing decision-making and driving career growth. 6. Adaptability Adaptability is the most relevant leadership skill, which can be developed by continuously learning about AI advancements, embracing the power of these changes and fostering an innovative culture. Since technology evolves rapidly, ongoing and frequent training is a must. This allows teams to fully embrace how AI can scale the workloads under ever-increasing consumer and business demands. 7. High-Level Communication Skills Artificial Intelligence is incredibly powerful and can help you find a solution or develop a plan quickly. What AI cannot do is employ emotional intelligence or utilize a variety of communication skills without excessive prompting. Leaders who have high emotional intelligence and advanced communication skills will be in demand in an era where anyone who knows how to use AI can appear qualified. - 8. Humility We all must accept that certain longtime aspects of our jobs will vanish in the face of AI. Embracing this, rather than fighting it, will help you to take advantage of the flip side of the coin: AI will help us work smarter and more efficiently, handling manual, tedious tasks and vastly helping with idealization. But we'll need to leave our egos at the door to fully take advantage.

9. **Mental Agility.**

Adaptability is key to thriving in an AI-driven world. Apply AI concepts to real-world projects, like pilot programs or projects that utilize AI tools. Embrace continuous learning by actively seeking new developments in AI. Cultivate an agile mindset, encourage innovation and stay open to change. Lead with empathy, guide teams through transitions and ensure AI enhances, not replaces, human talent. -

10. Knowledge Of When To Apply AI.

Understanding and applying AI to the right use cases or causes, in the right way, will help businesses. Always start with the "why" and "purpose" and then assess "fit," followed by the right application.

11. Prioritization Skills.

Along with several of the skills shared by fellow contributors, I'd add prioritization skills to the list in this age of AI. It's easy to get excited about all the new tools at our fingertips, but you need to prioritize and decide where you're going to invest first and truly deliver business impact. Trying to add AI to everything will likely lead to poor implementation and lackluster results.

12 Authenticity.

Leaders should focus on the ethical usage and application of AI, coupled with authenticity. In a world increasingly driven by AI, people value real involvement and in-person interactions. Authenticity builds trust and reliability, which are crucial as AI evolves. Developing these skills enhances career growth by addressing complex, people-driven business problems with empathy and trust.

13. Compassion And Understanding.

The art of leading with empathy and compassion will be critical in the future. Staff across all industries will feel the encroachment of AI on their roles. It is our job as leaders to allow team members to understand that it is important to embrace the future and be continuous learners. Leaders should be developing new skills that complement the introduction of AI in our careers, not trying to stop it. 14. An Understanding Of How AI Can Complement Human Skills. Leaders must develop soft skills to understand how to leverage AI strengths and complement them with the uniquely human skills of their workforce. Cultivate a mindset of collaboration over competition with AI. Identifying areas where AI can enhance human capabilities will be a pathway to the successful implementation of AI.

15 Timely, Action-Oriented Decision-Making.

The ability to interpret the data and make action-oriented decisions will be the most important skill for leaders in the age of artificial intelligence. Decisions like real-time pricing adjustments, real-time promotions and real-time placement will all be enhanced and executed with AI. Those who use AI to make faster, more informed and timely decisions will give their company a competitive advantage.

16 Relationship Building.

Relationships are the ultimate game-changer. Leaders who build strong connections can inspire teams, win deals and create loyal followers. AI can't replicate the magic of human bonds.

In the age of AI, fostering a culture that embraces fast failure and rapid innovation without fear is paramount. This leadership principle encourages agility and creativity. Leaders can develop this by promoting experimentation, learning from failures and providing psychological safety. Continuous learning and open communication are essential to expediting AI adoption and the realization of value. -

18. Strategic Thinking Skills.

In the age of artificial intelligence, strategic thinking is one of the most relevant leadership principles or skills. It enables leaders to navigate the complexities and opportunities extended by AI and other advanced technologies. Leaders can develop it through continuous learning, networking, improving analytical skills, encouraging innovation and leveraging AI tools and feedback loops. -

19. Coordination of Teams

Great leadership is more than just having a lot of followers; it is about managing and inspiring others. This rule remains the same: managers should use AI as a tool and capitalize on its potential, but not to the point where it takes the place of human perspectives and feelings. Not because of a tool or piece of technology in the leader's toolbox, but rather because they will see how committed their leader is to them, people will believe and support your goal.

20. 20. **Interpreting Data**

It is critical to comprehend and understand facts. Using data visualization tools and promoting data-driven decision-making within teams are also beneficial. One way that Amazon demonstrates this strategy is through requiring its executives to regularly use data to inform choices. In order to help leaders properly utilize AI findings, the organization also offers comprehensive training in data analytic.

Chapter 6

The laws of respect

It is human nature to follow those who are stronger than oneself.

People do not just happen to follow other people. They adhere to those whose leadership they value. On a scale of 1 to 10, where 10 is the strongest, those who are an 8 in leadership do not actively seek for a 6 to follow; instead, they naturally follow a 9 or 10. The gifted and more skillful lead the less skilled. People are generally drawn to leaders who are more capable than themselves. What makes one appreciate and adhere to another? Is it a result of the leader's attributes? Or is it because of the procedure they adhere to? or perhaps the situation? The top six strategies to assist leaders win others' respect are as follows, according to John Maxwell:

1. innate capacity for leadership

Individuals who are naturally gifted leaders will be drawn to you. They will desire to be in your presence. You can talk to them, and they will. They will get enthusiastic when you share your vision with them. However, keep in mind the Law of Solid Ground. Simply having talent is never sufficient. You will not be able to realize your full leadership potential and people might stop following you if you do not possess some of the extra behaviors and traits mentioned below. Relying just on talent is one of the biggest traps for natural leaders.

2. Consideration for other people

In order to get people to do what they want, dictators and other autocratic authorities resort to violence and intimidation. That is not how one leads. Honor is essential for good leaders. People follow leaders that they appreciate for their leadership.

3. Bravery

Effective leaders follow their moral convictions despite the possibility of failing, extreme peril, and unrelenting criticism. Courage in a leader is very valuable because it inspires optimism in others.

Outstanding leaders act morally.

4. Achievement

People honor the achievements of others. A strong record makes arguments difficult. People respect leaders who achieve success in their own pursuits. Many people are eager to learn from those who are successful in a certain field, especially in this day and age when people like to present themselves as bigger than they truly are. Which field do you excel in? Where can you motivate people to achieve success?

5. Faithfulness

Loyalty is a benefit in a society that is constantly changing, fluctuating, and transitioning. Followers respect leaders and their actions when they stay with the team until the task is completed, support the organization through difficult times, and look out for their followers even when it hurts them.

6. Worth added to other people

Leaders are most respected when they are committed to making a positive difference in the lives of others. Further information on this can be found here in the Law of Addition.

To gauge your level of respect as a leader, start by observing the people you surround yourself with. Observing how your people react to requests for commitment or change should be your second course of action.

People rise to the occasion when recognized leaders ask for commitment, and they get it. They are prepared to take chances, work longer hours, or do whatever else is required to finish the task at hand. Similarly, when well-respected leaders request change, their following are open to accepting it. I have had numerous experiences with it with my teams in various contexts and times.Individuals will always go over and above to back a leader they admire.

Individuals will always go above and beyond to back respected leaders.

But when disrespected leaders make demands for

commitment or change, people either ignore them or cast doubt on them. A leader who has not gained respect finds it extremely difficult to inspire others to follow them.

It is possible that you are trying to lead people whose leadership is weaker than your own if you have ever felt upset because the people you want to follow you won't.

How can you address this?Improve as a leader!A leader who aspires to improve can never run out of hope. Additionally, the better people you attract, the more you will grow. because followers of stronger leaders tend to follow them by nature.

The law of solid ground

The Law of Solid Ground: Trust is the foundation of a through leadership. Trust is the glue that holds an organization together. Leaders cannot repeatedly break trust with people and continue to influence them. Trust is the foundation of leadership. No matter what country you live in, what organization you are part of or what religion you belong to. If you don't earn trust of your people, you can't influence them. Growing up in communist country, I've seen people in position using power to scare people into doing things they wanted them to do. This is not the high level leadership we're discussing here. Yes, it's much easier to scare people into obedience or force them into action you desire. But beware, their hearts won't follow. When it comes to leadership, you can't take shortcuts, no matter how long you've been leading people. Decisions need to be done the right way. John Maxwell compares trust to change in a leader's pocket. Each time you make good leadership decisions, you earn more change. Each time you make poor decisions, you pay out some of your change to the people. Whatever you do either builds up your change or depletes it. If you make one bad decision after another, you keep paying out change. Then one day, after making one last bad decision, you suddenly run out of change. When you're out of change, you're out as the leader. How does a leader build trust? By consistently exemplifying competence, connection, and character. People will forgive you occasional mistakes, especially if you're new and still in a learning process. But they won't overlook flaws in your character. Whenever you lead people, it's like you take them on a journey with you. The quality of the trip is predicted by your character. With good character, the longer the trip, the better it seems. But if your character is flawed, the longer the trip, the worse it gets. Why? Because no one enjoys spending time with someone they don't trust. There are many things your character communicates to others. Let's have a look at the top three:

1. Consistency.

Leaders without good character can't be counted on day after day because their ability to perform changes constantly. If you want to become a great leader, you need to learn the art of consistency. Always give your best in spite of circumstances. Consistency builds trust. If people know that you can be trusted no matter what happens, they will follow your lead.

2. Potential Poor character is like a time bomb ticking away. It's only a matter of time before it blows up a persona's ability to perform and the capacity to lead. Talent is never enough. We've seen many talented people fade because of their character flaws. If you want to go far and above as a leader, remember that the journey starts with you. Be honest with yourself and choose to improve your character. Invest in yourself! Not just your skills and knowledge, but your character. Start with these three areas: integrity, authenticity and discipline. •Integrity - make a commitment to yourself to be brutally honest. Don't shave the truth, don't tell white lies, don't tweak the numbers. Be truthful even when it hurts. •Authenticity - discover yourself and choose to be yourself with everyone. Stop pretending to be who you

are not. •Discipline - do the right things every day regardless of how you feel. Choose to not die without making the most out of what's been given to you!

3. Respect.

Respect is not a given. It's not a right. You can't demand it. You earn it. You earn it the hard way on a regular continual basis. Leaders earn respect by making sound decisions, admitting their mistakes and by putting what's best for their followers (organization) ahead of their personal agendas. One more comment on the topic of respect. There's a difference between respect and honor. We honor people for what they've done in the past. Respect is for what you're doing today. It's better to have respect than honor! Wake up every morning ready to earn respect.

Dr Stella Hill

Chapter 7

Become a Stronger and More Effective Leader (Law of Process)

Develop Into a More Powerful and Successful Leader (Law of Process).

When it comes to adopting new habits in their lives, most people will give it anywhere from three hours to three weeks. Many of them give up since they do not notice any effects. Before it manifests on the outside, growth occurs internally. Essentially, something does not always stop working just because you can not see it.

It takes time to develop into a stronger, more capable leader. The Law of Process, the third of John Maxwell's 21 Irrefutable Laws of Leadership, asserts that leadership develops throughout time, not just once.

Every year, I have the honor of working with hundreds of organizational executives as a trainer, speaker, and leadership coach. Many people think they are leaders just because they read a book, attend a conference, or take part in one of our leadership calls.

As a result of their patience and self-control, successful leaders are in fact lifelong learners. "Microwave leaders do not have any staying power," as John Maxwell once stated. Being a leader is more like cooking in a crock pot. Although it takes time, the result is well worth the wait. You will eventually experience growth if you make consistent investments in your leadership development.

Be Prepared for Confidence

"Champions do not become champions in the ring—they are merely recognized there," goes an old proverb. Look at someone is daily routine to determine where they get their champion status. Even those with innate skill and aptitude need to practice. This past year, more than thirty charter school principals engaged in our leadership development program, the Regional Principal Consortium, to watch high-performing schools such as Henderson Collegiate Charter School in Vance County, NC, and their best practices. After attending our program, a principal came back to report that she had seen a teacher purposefully and passionately instructing to an empty classroom.

"Yes, you will see that pretty often here," the founder, Eric Sanchez, replied with a smile in response to her remark. Henderson Collegiate is one of the best performing Title I schools in North Carolina and has outperformed academic gains for five years running, in large part because of this deliberate application of the "Law of Process."

This makes perfect sense to me as a former high school coach and collegiate baseball player. We consistently and intensely drilled the fundamentals of baseball every day. We deliberately placed gamer in high-stress scenarios so they would be prepared for the inevitable. When it came time for the game, we thought you would not be able to just switch it on.

Direct instruction was the primary teaching strategy used in elementary schools when I served as principal. Our primary school teachers trained as leaders by working with coaches. Maintaining a steady pace and rhythm was essential to guaranteeing a high degree of participation. However, in the middle school, we did not have such precision in our education plan and instructional methods

Knowledge modifies perceptions; altering one's perspective modifies behavior.

When I was a principal's coach, I would ask, "During which section of the training will they be practicing that skill? " in response to any inquiry about how her teachers were improving. Who will provide them with feedback and how frequently will they practice?

You may apply the concept of practice to every area of your life. Prepare your pitch if you are in charge of sales. To perfect an eight-minute speech, professional speakers put in hundreds of hours of practice. For months, comedians rehearse and test their material in the most unlikely settings in order to be ready for that 45-minute show.

When was the last time you dedicated practice time to improving upon something you truly value?

We run leadership teams' mastermind book studies and training's as a leadership development organization. I enjoy seeing the group develop across these five learning stages:

First Phase: I am Not Sure What I Do not Know Not many people consider themselves to be leaders. A person will not consciously develop as long as he does not understand how crucial leadership is to success in general.

Phase 2: I Know that I Need to Know – We will eventually realize that if we want to live better lives, we must learn how to lead. I refer to this stage as "Failing Forward."

Phase 3: I Am Aware of My Unknowns If we do not develop better at becoming leaders, our careers will eventually stagnate. You create a strategy for personal development in the areas where you still need work during this phase.

Phase 4: Knowledge and Development Begin to Show Exciting things start to happen when you acknowledge your areas of weakness and commit to the daily discipline of personal growth. You begin to develop into a capable leader, but you still need to consider each decision you make.

Phase 5: I Just Proceed Based on My Knowledge You develop a near-automatic ability to lead. You have wonderful insights that lead to amazing rewards, but the only way to get there is to follow the "Law of Process" and be willing to put in countless hours of sacrifice and hard work.

Grow as a Leader: What will set you apart from your followers is your ability to acquire and enhance your skills.

Personal development is a never-ending game. Personal improvement is an ongoing process.

Write down your answers to the following three questions, then make a plan to grow by 1% a week for the next twelve months. You will be fifty percent better than when you started, even after taking a two-week vacation.

1. Consider your location this day one year ago. What factor most contributed to your development as a leader? Make a weekly strategy to double that time.

2. Check the schedule for the day. What deliberate

actions are you taking today to improve tomorrow? Cross off everything on your calendar that will not help you reach your objective.

3. How is your group improving as a leadership team? Start investing in your team by sharing your lessons with them every week.

What difficulties are you and the company currently facing?

What worries you so much at night?

What difficulties and barriers do they anticipate in the upcoming six to twelve months that might put the team's weaknesses to the test? What is it that they personally find difficult to overcome this obstacle?

When their organization is performing at its best, how does it look and feel?

What does your definition of personal success entail?

The Lid Law.

According to the Law of the Lid, your efficacy and chances of success are based on your leadership skills. Fundamentally, the Law of the Lid suggests that our capacity for leadership sets a lid or ceiling on our potential. The lid is high if our leadership abilities are strong. However, if we have poor leadership qualities, this low ceiling caps us and reduces our chances of success as well.

For instance, if a person's leadership skill is rated a 4 on a scale of 1 to 10, their effectiveness, success, and influence will never exceed a 4. They need to develop their leadership skills and raise the lid on their leadership potential. A person's potential is higher the more capable he is as a leader.

This idea emphasizes how crucial it is to keep improving one's leadership skills in order to increase one's chances of success. It highlights how important it is for leaders to continuously make investments in their own leadership development in order to expand their skill set and become more capable leaders.

Microsoft, led by Bill Gates, is a prime example of this

law. His innovative management approach propelled Microsoft to previously unheard-of heights in the computer sector.

Dr Stella Hill

Chapter 8

Rules for good leadership

I have had the privilege of working closely with several prominent scientists throughout the years. I refer to these as individuals who oversee their own laboratories, departments, and schools within universities, national laboratories, and funding bodies such as the National Institutes of Health (NIH), collectively referred to as organizations. There are eminent scientists who hold several academy memberships, national medals, and Nobel Prizes. Why are some of them effective leaders? My response is individualized and subjective. Observe the mention of "some of them." Although there is some correlation, being a competent scientist does not always translate into being a good leader, especially in this day and age where science is a team sport needing a variety of knowledge that needs to be led. Similarly, having strong leadership qualities does not always equate to having strong management qualities. Thought leaders are fine, but they must also be able to assign managerial responsibilities.

I would broadly divide leaders into two categories: enabling and autocratic. Unexpectedly, both can be successful in terms of the organizations they run, but autocrats make the workplace—whether it be a smaller or larger organization—much less enjoyable for people who carry out the organization's tasks. The guidelines for becoming an enabling leader—a person who thinks that the organization benefits most when individuals do well—are as follows. I have given an example from my personal observations that best illustrates each rule.

First Rule: **Set an Example**.

You can not hold somebody to standards that you would not hold yourself to. You must put in more hours of work if you want other people to put in lengthier hours. You must fulfill deadlines yourself if you want others to do the same, and so on. Setting a good example makes you respected for the work you accomplish on behalf of the company. Being respected is a prerequisite for effective leadership, and it must be gained over time. After receiving high praise for his speech at my institution the previous evening, a respected leader came to stay at our home. They were going to speak with me by the fire that day in front of a live audience. Were they dozing off while reveling in the previous night's happenings? No, they were not up until after sunrise working on their daily tasks before this extra activity. It is evident that witnessing such commitment stays with one.

Rule 2: Have humility.

A competent leader helps create a successful organization; they are not the only thing. Acknowledge that and act modestly. There must be individuals in your organization who are more intelligent and skilled in specific areas than you are if you want to create something truly remarkable. It is impossible to excel in every endeavor. Acknowledge this while praising and rewarding people for the abilities they contribute to the company. You will get respect from your team for it. Give credit where credit is due and do not hoard for yourself. Say "we" as much as you can, rather than "I." If you lead an organization well and are humble, credit will find its way to you. Being modest and honorable, a Nobel Laureate I know will not put their name on the publication unless they believe they have made a major practical scientific contribution to the work at hand, even though they are endorsing the science.

Rule 3: Show Equity, Inclusion, and Personality.
Everyone enjoys receiving praise or other forms of acknowledgment. Why would not others do as you and I do? Accurately acknowledging someone is contribution and making sure to mention everyone who contributed are crucial when calling someone out. Don't, however, give it too much attention because that will lessen its significance.

Acknowledging the person is the first step towards inclusion, and it starts with their name. I have witnessed outstanding leaders introduce themselves to twenty people in a room and recall each person's name without taking notes. Even when you have to write down their name and then look it up, addressing someone by name shows how valuable they are—even if some of us lack that skill. Knowing individuals for who they are, not simply what they do for the organization, goes beyond knowing their names. The human/personal touch is crucial. Learn as much as you can about the people you work with as coworkers—people with unique personalities, families, and histories. Maintain objectivity. Every team member should be treated equally in every element of running the company.

Rule 4: Utilize Shared Governance and Consensus to Lead.

Autocrats often rule by decree, making others feel unimportant or, at most, undervalued. Seeking input from a wide range of individuals within the organization, enabling leaders operate by consensus or, in the event that they deviate from the consensus, provide a clear and honest explanation for their actions. When they met with the job candidate at the end of the day, a well-known leader I know would make sure they had the opinions of every interviewee. That information would be taken into consideration right away when deciding whether to recruit this individual. One such person who was employed in this manner was me.

Rule 5: Show Consideration .

An organization is defined by its people. People are cared for by good leaders. It follows that the top companies are able to draw in and keep the best employees because word of mouth spreads. Being compassionate, listening to people who look up to you as a leader, and showing empathy for other people's problems and family situations are all examples of caring. COVID has increased the significance of this strategy.

Being compassionate benefits the leader as much as the organization. One instance that comes to mind for me personally is when I was a candidate for a leadership post and a former student who is now a professor was on the search committee. His support was unaffected by our previous connection because I had mentored him successfully, but it is likely that my caring was recognized by him personally, which added significantly to my value to the company.

Rule 6: Have a clear vision .

People in the company will look to you for direction. The organization's definition will be greatly influenced by your vision. If executed correctly, it will seem like a group vision. Everyone in the company will experience a sense of ownership over the creation of the vision. In a way, your duty is to seed the idea and empower others to develop, nourish and promote the vision as their own. Here is where strategic strategies come into play. They provide a path for everyone to take. When people claim your vision as their own and you are proud of them for doing so, you will have succeeded. Adoption is the best recommendation.

Following their appointment, our university's new president and provost began creating a strategic plan, which required a great deal of work to gather input from all stakeholders through surveys, town halls, and other venues (see Rule 3). Then, that alleged "2030 strategy" was reduced to the simple phrase "Be Both Great and Good." I, along with many other stakeholders, use the phrase on a regular basis. a succinct declaration of their organization's vision that is understood by all.

Rule 7: Make a Decision

Making decisions as a leader can be difficult at times. Decisions are not always obvious, and decisions will have an effect on individuals and the organization. That means there has to be a risk-taking component. Making decisions should be based on what you think is best for the organization, not on how you think other members of the organization will respond to them. Making no choice at all and leaving the organization in a condition of indecision is worse. Sometimes, even the best leaders will make poor choices. The most crucial thing to keep in mind is to collaborate with all parties involved to achieve a good conclusion and to be open and honest with them about the reasoning behind decisions taken. It is crucial to own up to your mistakes and promptly make the necessary corrections after consulting with your teammates.

One instance that I have witnessed frequently is recruiting. The leader must decide who gets hired if the search committee and other parties disagree. Not being decisive enough could result in both candidates leaving for other positions, but having to make a decision will risk upsetting half of your stakeholders. A competent leader considers every aspect of both candidates and solicits feedback from all relevant parties. They clearly communicate the decision-making process and demand respect from all parties when the candidate they did not select joins the team.

Rule 8: Assemble the Correct Groups and Allow Them to Choose the Route .

Arguably the most significant guideline, this one suggests that you should be careful who you choose to work with. Individuals define the organization, as I have stated. Selecting the appropriate candidates for your company is crucial. One misfit employee has the power to negatively impact the entire small business. Both organizations and science benefit greatly from innovation. Allow your team members to be creative. Avoid being overly restrictive as this may hinder intelligent individuals. Be flexible yourself as well. You might not follow the route you had intended to travel. If they lack the drive or personality to contribute to the success of the company, even the most intelligent candidates with the highest qualifications might not be the best ones to hire. In a scientific institution where individual contributions are valued, this is a delicate balance. To do it properly, it might take some mistakes.

The proper people will, as mentioned, be more intelligent than you. Such individuals will be difficult for the autocratic leader to hire, which results in businesses that are not at their best and have turned away the brightest employees.

I moved on when a fantastic boss I worked for did not provide me the position I desired. They followed all the regulations here, though, so even at first I admired their choice. As I continued to watch the candidate who was hired, I came to the conclusion that I would not have been the greatest fit, which would have prevented both the organization and I from working to our full potential.

Rule 9: Assign

Everything is beyond your reach. This is increasingly evident when a company expands. You must surround yourself with a sufficient number of direct reports that you have complete faith in to carry out the organization's tasks. This is true even for small individual labs where more senior and experienced members assume leadership roles as the lab grows.

The director will have a small number of deputy directors and the dean will have a small number of associate deans as direct reports in a larger institution, like a university or funding agency. These deputy leaders in highly functional businesses trust and value these deputies, and their diverse skill sets complement the organization as a whole.

Rule 10: Enjoy the Experience but Know When to Stop. It spreads when someone is happy with their position inside the company. How can others be motivated by what you are doing if it does not inspire you? You are either not suited for the position or you are not leading the proper kind of organization if you are not having fun in your role as a leader. You must pose these challenging questions to yourself. Your enjoyment could also have a time component. Leading a small organization is different from turning a small organization into a large one and leading that. Recognize when to arrive and when to depart.

Before I started this project myself, I had the wonderful fortune to observe a brilliant leader establish a new school within a major university. That leader followed these ten guidelines, but he also knew when to give up. By doing this, they created a team that would carry on and established a succession plan that would ensure the company carried on when they were gone. Hopefully, I have also learned that lesson.

There you have it. It is never too early to begin considering a career in leadership. There are countless leadership books, films, and courses available. They might have more insightful leadership tips to give you.

Dr Stella Hill

Chapter 9

conclusion.

Developing as a leader necessitates a purposeful dedication to self-improvement and the comprehension of fundamental leadership concepts. The nine laws of leadership, which are self-awareness, emotional intelligence, compassion, teamwork, and trust-building, offer prospective leaders a strong platform on which to realize their greatest potential. People who live by these laws not only become better leaders, but they also encourage and uplift people around them.

If you are interested in implementing this highly effective strategy but do not know where to begin, consider enrolling in Aventine "The 5 Laws of Leadership to

Emerge as a Leader" course. Daniel Lee, the author of the book "First Time Leadership," will walk you through the process in a highly practical one-day workshop. You will undoubtedly obtain insightful knowledge of these concepts, enabling you to become a leader who encourages, inspires, and leads others toward mutual accomplishment.

Just before we wrap up this article, keep in mind that becoming a leader is an ongoing process of learning and development. Accept these rules, set an example, and see the extraordinary leader that God has created within you.

www.ingramcontent.com/pod-product-compliance
Lightning Source LLC
Chambersburg PA
CBHW071058240526
45471CB00016B/1993